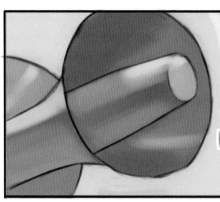

MEN'S SURF COMPETITION!

LAST CALL FOR REGISTRATION!

Knew I forgot something.

You're not signed up?

No. I forgot to tell them --

-- I'm donating my winnings --

-- to the Orange County Disabled Foundation.

Makes me feel almost guilty about kicking his ...

Hey! I saw Pooja arrive -- with your brother.

Oh?

Goof, he had his arm around her!

Scandalous!

A yellow Karman Ghia is blocking a loading zone ...

YAARRGHHH!

HEE-HEE-HEE!

Back track to breakfast...

He probably would.

He thinks all females are useless.

So . . .

You want me to be Pooja's camera man.

Not all females. Just kid sisters.

Recycle much?

Only when Mom is looking.

I thought
this was
top of
the line.

It is,
Pooja.

Hey! I thought
you didn't know
how to use that?

=giggle=
Who
says?

How -- how did I...?

Zach brought you here.

You were at a club. Alone. And feeling no pain, apparently.

DING-DONG

OH, NO! IT'S BEAU!

GASP!

Mom! Who called him ?!?!?

Where'dja park this time? In a fire lane?

Jerkhead moved his car. I parked in the lot.

C'mon. He's not so bad.

I don't see Joplin.

This is his event. Where is he?

...uh, he must not know it's starting...

You guys wait for him here. I'll have a look around.

Save me a spot!

C'mon, J. Get in the game.

Why?

So Pooch can record your victory!

WHOOHOO!

GO, JOPLIN!

YEAH!

Glad you could make it, Mrs. Hendrix.

Me too.

Flying back to Milan tonight?

Nope . . . They'll just have to cope without me.

It must be exciting, running a modeling agency.

It's also demanding. And not very nice.

What do you look for in a model?

What you'd expect.

. . . and something more, something hard to define . . .

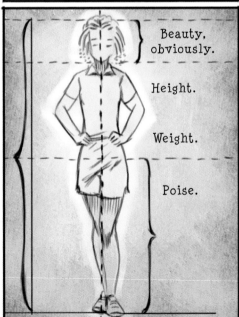

Beauty, obviously.

Height.

Weight.

Poise.

Like **that** girl.

. . . oy gevalt . . .

Do you know her?

Uh, no. Joplin does, though.

Reeeeeeeeeally?

Gotta go.

Game two! Take your positions, Team Red!

We'll talk after I win!

Hello.

I'm Joplin's mother.

I run an agency. Call me.

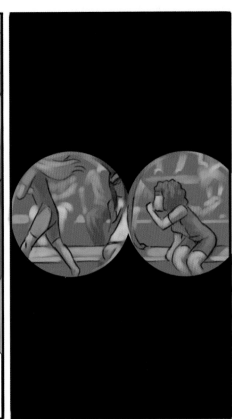

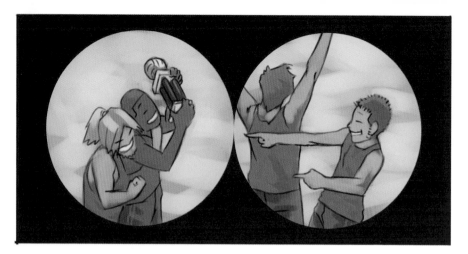

Team captain Joplin Hendrix is a one-man winning machine. Next up: women's surfing.

Remember what I told you, Suki.

HellooOOoo?

In here!

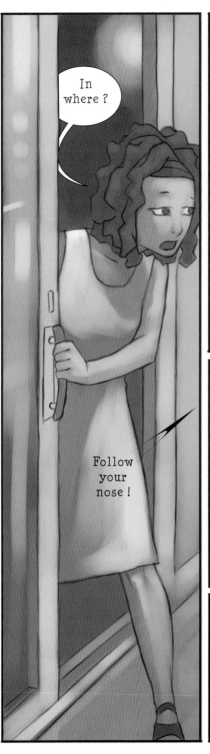

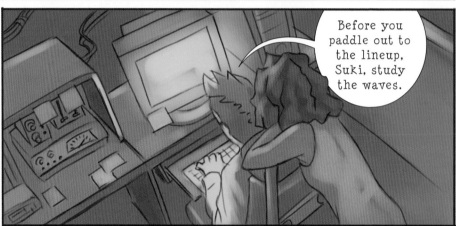

TOLDJA YOU COULD DO IT!

That was fantastic!

Desert on the deck?

Oh, later, please. I'm stuffed.

Leave it. I'll do it later.

Do you have help?

I want to show you something. Some pointers for the contest tomorrow.

You're using a short board?

My vintage speed egg.

Those 12-footers require the duck-dive.

Bottom turn after the drop to get into the pocket.

Pay attention to the form on those speed cuts.

Effortless bomb back down!

You know a lot about this.

Where was this video shot?

Mexico. Salsipuedes. Five years ago.

Heh, heh. Salsipuedes. "Exit, **if** you can."

That's you, isn't it?

Dinner and a movie.

I've ridden other things beside this chair, Suki.

Take it. Study it tonight. It'll help tomorrow, believe me.

Okay.

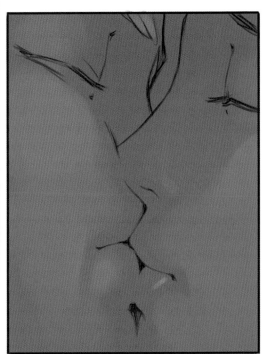

No !
The men's
competition
is last !

Lots of people here for the men's surfing event !

Narrating her video as she shoots.

Emergency crews . . .

. . . Coast Guard hunks . . .

It's a perfect day !

HEY !

I'm getting a disturbance on my Doppler . . .

Disturbance ?

I've seen it before. Rogue wave.

Not getting that, sir.

Not getting . . . ?

Conditions are good. No reports of . . .

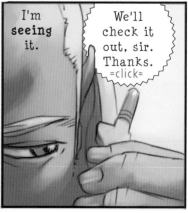

I'm **seeing** it.

We'll check it out, sir. Thanks. =click=

He left with his mom!

Are we waiting for Joplin?

And Fifi.

"Fifi"?

A new nemesis.

deedle
leedle
deedle
leedle

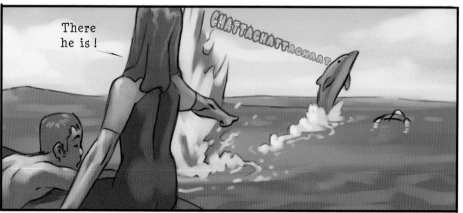

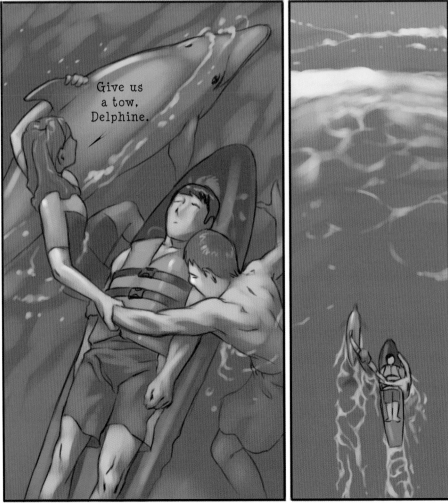

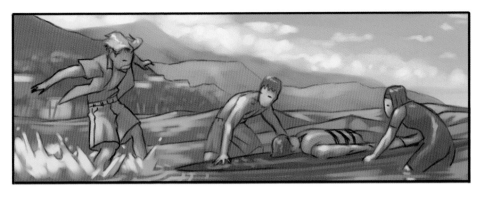

Looks like the danger's over. Not sure what happened . . .

. . . but the Coast Guard warns everyone to stay out of the water. . .

...No winner in the men's competition...

I wouldn't say that ... Scott, keep the board . . .

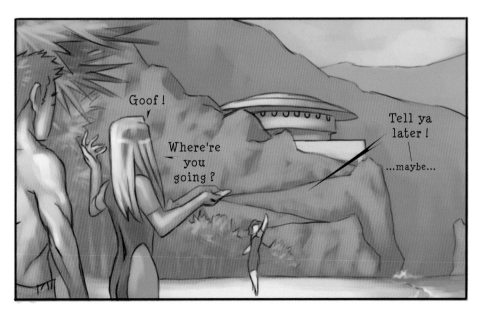

Good work, 007.

Me? **You're** the action figure.

That wave! The Coast Guard didn't even see it coming.

Let me show you a little something I developed.

The Coast Guard doesn't have these: Sensors to read changes in wave patterns.

The Indonesian tsunami inspired it. Tragically. I wanted to test them.

They
worked.

Zip, this could
save lives.

That's
the general
idea.

How
did you test
them?

I
have my
ways.

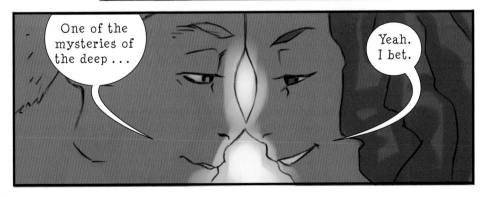

It starts with an
INNOCENT
QUESTION...

...that leads to a
CHALLENGE...

...that becomes
an OBSESSION...

...and finally
EXPLODES
in
ANGER!

It's

LIFE !
CAMERA !
ACTION !

starring

Serenity !

While "Life !" goes on, everybody's favorite blue-haired oddball and her friends turn their energy and talents behind the "Camera !" to make "Action !" movies with a decidedly different perspective !

Coming Soon from Thomas Nelson and Realbuzz Studios - four BRAND NEW Serenity stories !

Serenity Vol. 7

Space Cadet vs. Drama Queen

Serenity Vol. 8

Sunday Best

Serenity Vol. 9

Choosing Change

Serenity Vol. 10

Girl Overboard

...and featuring these "movies" !

For more info visit
www.SerenityBuzz.com
www.RealbuzzStudios.com

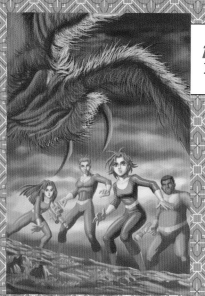

TERROR FROM THE TARANTULA NEBULA
Deep space voyagers discover
a sinister secret!

CRAWLING FROM THE WRECKAGE
All exits blocked!
Earthquake at the mall!

ESTHER, QUEEN OF PERSIA
A Biblical epic of romance
and intrigue!

FRAULEIN STEIN'S MONSTER
Monster mayhem marks
a remarkable revelation!

Hey, folks! They're not really "movies" - they're stories that READ like movies!

THE revolve TOUR

Hawk Nelson

ALL NEW **EVENT** for Teen Girls
PRESENTED BY WOMEN OF FAITH

Natalie Grant

KJ-52

We're Coming to a City Near You!
TOUR DATES

Columbus, OH
September 14 - 15, 2007

Dallas, TX
September 21 - 22, 2007

Hartford, CT
September 28 - 29, 2007

St. Louis, MO
October 5 - 6, 2007

Anaheim, CA
October 12 - 13, 2007

Sacramento, CA
October 19 - 20, 2007

Philadelphia, PA
November 2 - 3, 2007

Minneapolis, MN
November 9 - 10, 2007

Portland, OR
November 16 - 17, 2007

Atlanta, GA
November 30 - Dec. 1, 2007

Orlando, FL
January 25 - 26, 2008

Charlotte, NC
February 1 - 2, 2008

Denver, CO
February 15 - 16, 2008

Houston, TX
February 22 - 23, 2008

Max & Jenna Lucado

Ayiesha Woods

Chad Eastham
Kimiko Soldati

Download **Preview Video** Online

To register by phone, call 877-9-REVOLVE
or online at REVOLVETOUR.COM

Goofyfoot Gurl

Hot Dogger: Tony Weinstock
Wahine: Allison Barrows
Big kahuna: Realbuzz Studios
Shakas To: George B., David K., Chiz C.,
the irrepressable Thom B., and all the crew at GNH

Copyright © 2007 by Realbuzz Studios, Inc.   ISBN 1595543929 / 9781595543929

Published by Thomas Nelson, Inc. Nashville, TN 37214 www.thomasnelson.com

Library of Congress Cataloguing-in-Publication Data
Applied For

Printed in Singapore.
5 4 3 2 1

VISIT GOOFYFOOT GURL AT:
www.RealbuzzStudios.com